W9-BKU-754

Festivals of the World

FINLAND

Gareth Stevens Publishing
MILWAUKEE

Written by
TAN CHUNG LEE

Edited by
AUDREY LIM

Designed by
LOO CHUAN MING

Picture research by
SUSAN JANE MANUEL

First published in North America in 1998 by
Gareth Stevens Publishing
1555 North RiverCenter Drive, Suite 201
Milwaukee, Wisconsin 53212 USA

For a free color catalog describing Gareth
Stevens' list of high-quality books and multimedia
programs, call
1-800-542-2595 (USA)
or 1-800-461-9120 (Canada).
Gareth Stevens Publishing's Fax: (414) 225-0377.
See our catalog, too, on the World Wide Web:
http://gsinc.com

All rights reserved. No part of this book may be
reproduced or utilized in any form or by any
means electronic or mechanical, including
photocopying, recording, or by an information
storage and retrieval system, without permission
from the copyright owner.

© **TIMES EDITIONS PTE LTD 1998**
Originated and designed by
Times Books International
an imprint of Times Editions Pte Ltd
Times Centre, 1 New Industrial Road
Singapore 536196
Printed in Singapore

Library of Congress Cataloging-in-Publication Data:
Tan, Chung Lee.
Finland / by Tan Chung Lee.
p. cm.—(Festivals of the world)
Includes bibliographical references and index.
Summary: Describes how the culture of Finland is
reflected in the celebration of festivals throughout
the year, including Midsummer Festival,
Pikkujoulu, Shrove Tuesday, and Students' Day.
ISBN 0-8368-2013-4 (lib. bdg.)
1. Festivals—Finland—Juvenile literature. 2.
Finland—Social life and customs—Juvenile
literature. [1. Festivals—Finland. 2. Holidays—
Finland. 3. Finland—Social life and customs.]
I. Title. II. Series.
GT4871.F6T36   1998
394.2694897—dc21   97-52102

1 2 3 4 5 6 7 8 9 02 01 00 99 98

CONTENTS

It's Festival Time . . .

Finns are quiet when you first meet them, but they can be warm when they get to know you. And do they love to party! They enjoy wearing their national costumes at festivals, especially when celebrating Midsummer. They also love to dance, and they enjoy special food and drinks. So come on and join the Finns as they celebrate their festivals all year round.

WHERE'S FINLAND?

inland lies in the northern region of the world. It is the twelfth largest country in Europe. However, it has one of Europe's smallest populations. Finland's neighbors are Sweden to the west, Norway to the north, and Russia to the east.

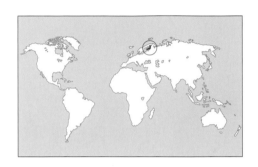

Who are the Finns?

These two boys certainly look pleased with their catch! How would you cook this giant fish?

Ten thousand years ago, the Sami, or Lapps, arrived in Finland from Asia. They herded reindeer across Norway, Sweden, Finland, and Russia. Then about 2,000 years ago, immigrants from Hungary and Estonia settled in Finland. Later, the Germanic tribes from the south of Europe came. In 1154, when Swedish settlers set out to fight in the **Crusades** in the Holy Land, they made Finland part of Sweden for 700 years. Today, 6 percent of Finland's people are Swedish in origin.

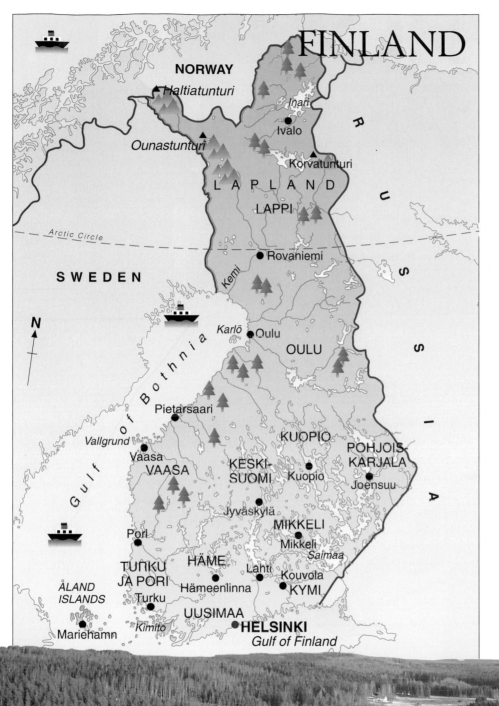

FINLAND

NORWAY

▲ *Haltiatunturi*

Inari

● Ivalo

Ounastunturi ▲

▲ Korvatunturi

L A P L A N D
LAPPI

R
U
S
S
I
A

Arctic Circle

SWEDEN

● Rovaniemi

Kemi

N

G
u
l
f

o
f

B
o
t
h
n
i
a

Karlö ● Oulu

OULU

● Pietarsaari

Vallgrund

● Vaasa
VAASA

KUOPIO

**KESKI-
SUOMI**

● Kuopio

**POHJOIS-
KARJALA**

● Joensuu

● Pori

● Jyväskylä

MIKKELI

● Mikkeli

Salmaa

**TURKU
JA PORI**

HÄME

● Hämeenlinna

● Lahti

● Kouvola

KYMI

*ÅLAND
ISLANDS*

● Turku

UUSIMAA

Kimito

● Mariehamn

● **HELSINKI**
Gulf of Finland

Finland is a land of
lakes—about
188,000 of them.
This is Aulanko Lake
in Hämeenlinna.
Two-thirds of the
country is covered
by forest.

WHEN'S THE PARTY?

Isn't my May Day costume colorful? Come join me in all the parties and celebrations!

SPRING

- ✪ **PALM SUNDAY**
- ✪ **GOOD FRIDAY**
- ✪ **EASTER**
- ✪ **EVE OF MAY DAY**—To celebrate the arrival of spring, people take to the streets or dance halls to dance. They also go to restaurants to have special meals with friends. Children drink a special lemonade called *sima* [SEE-ma] that is flavored with raisins.
- ✪ **MAY DAY**—The Finns call this first day in May *vappuaamuna* [va-po-AAH-mo-na], and it is greeted by choirs singing the joys of spring. Children join their parents to eat a traditional May Day lunch of fish, and they also watch a street carnival later.
  - ✪ **STUDENTS' DAY**—Celebrated on the evening of May Day by students to welcome spring.

SUMMER

- ✪ **MIDSUMMER FESTIVAL**—*Juhannus* [you-HA-nose] is a time for Finnish children and their parents to spend time in the countryside. *Juhannuskoko* [you-HA-nose-ko-KO], or midsummer bonfires, are lit around midnight. People dance and party outdoors. This is one time of the year when children can go to bed late!

Spring is a lovely time in Finland! Turn the pages and you'll see why!

AUTUMN

- ✪ **ALL SAINTS' DAY**—A time for families to remember loved ones who have passed away. People visit their graves to place wreaths.
- ✪ **PIKKUJOULU**—"Little Christmas" takes place as early as October. There are small parties, and people get together to prepare for Christmas.

WINTER

- ✪ **INDEPENDENCE DAY**
- ✪ **LUCIA DAY**
- ✪ **CHRISTMAS**
- ✪ **SAINT STEPHEN'S DAY**
- ✪ **NEW YEAR'S DAY**—Like new year celebrations everywhere, this is a time for partying, setting off fireworks, and making resolutions. It is also a time for fortune-telling.
- ✪ **FRIENDSHIP DAY**—The Finns call it *Ystavanpaiva* [OOH-sta-VAN PA-ee-va]. It takes place on February 14th. Children send special cards and stamps to one another to express their friendship.
- ✪ **SHROVE TUESDAY**

Whee! See how fast we are going down the slope! Be sure to dress warmly when you join us for Christmas!

EASTER

In Finland, Easter is a special festival. One reason is because with Easter comes the arrival of spring! To help them know if spring is near, children plant rye seeds several weeks before Easter in small pots or plates. The seed containers are then placed on windowsills to catch as much sunlight as possible. When grass begins to grow from the rye seeds, the children know spring has arrived.

Above: On Shrove Tuesday, children eat special treats like this Shrove Tuesday bun. It is filled with whipped cream. Yummy!

Below: See how much fun these children are having going down the slopes!

Shrove Tuesday

Seven weeks before Easter on Shrove Tuesday, children go tobogganing in the snow with their friends. Shrove Tuesday was previously celebrated to mark the end of a season of hard work on the farms. People enjoyed themselves by feasting and going tobogganing. Today, although fewer people in Finland farm for a living, children still repeat traditional poems wishing for enormous turnips and plenty of **flax**.

Shh! It is silent week

During Easter, children paint eggs and make chicks from cotton wool. These items are placed next to a vase of willow twigs.

"Silent week" starts with Palm Sunday and continues with Good Friday and Holy Saturday. Finally, it ends with Easter Sunday and Easter Monday. On Palm Sunday, friends and relatives gently whisk one another with willow twigs to wish each other good luck. At the end of the week, they make up for whisking each other by giving treats, eggs, or a coin.

Above: Even when this witch flies on her broomstick, she takes care never to leave the Easter eggs behind!

Flying witches

The Finns once believed witches flew around at night on broomsticks between Good Friday and Easter Sunday. These witches were old women who had sold their souls to the devil, and they flew around looking for people or animals to harm. People lit bonfires on Holy Saturday to scare the witches away.

Right: These two girls are dressed as witches. What do you think of their costumes?

Witches who wish you good luck

Today, witches are considered good luck symbols. At Easter, girls and boys dress up as witches. They blacken their faces with soot and go around from house to house with broomsticks and willow twigs to whisk people and wish them good luck. They recite poems and receive chocolates and sweets in return.

This is what mammi looks like. It's very delicious with sugar and cream.

A sweet treat

One of the most traditional sweets eaten at Easter is *mammi* [mum-mee]. This is a dark brown porridge of water and sweetened rye malt. The dessert is baked in cardboard boxes, which are decorated to look like birch bark baskets, and baked in a slow oven. Mammi is eaten with cream and sugar.

An Easter poem

At Easter, children go around wishing their parents, grandparents, and godparents good health by whisking them with decorated willow twigs. At the same time, they recite the following poem:

> "Gently whisking you with my twig,
> So that you may have good health in the coming year.
> Please, then, take this twig
> and give me a token sum in return."

The children usually receive chocolates or other candy in return for their good wishes.

Think about this

What day of the year do children in the United States dress up in witches' costumes to visit homes and receive chocolates and other sweet treats? Besides getting dressed as witches, what other costumes do they wear? When the occupant of the house opens the door to welcome them, what do the children say as a greeting? What is the name of this festival?

MIDSUMMER

C an you imagine having days when the sun hardly ever sets, and it is bright even at night? This happens in Finland during June and July. This season is called Midsummer or *juhannus* [you-HA-nose]. The nights are so bright the Finns call them white nights.

The sun shines brightly even at night during Midsummer in Finland. It is an amazing sight!

Land of the Midnight Sun

The eve of Midsummer Day falls on June 21st. On this day in Lapland, at the farthest corner of Finland, above the Arctic Circle, the sun never sets. This is why Lapland is also called the Land of the Midnight Sun.

These two children are from the Land of the Midnight Sun. People from Lapland are called Samis, or Lapps. Don't their festive outfits look bright and colorful?

Holiday activities

Summer is a happy time for the Finns. Finnish children are especially delighted because it is a time for vacations. Everyone in the family gets together to go to the countryside and enjoy themselves. Many families have a vacation home, usually a log cabin, near a lake. Here they spend time fishing or boating, and picking all kinds of berries in the forest. Other favorite activities the Finns enjoy during Midsummer include **canoeing** and sailing on the lakes, and hiking.

Above: These two children are enjoying their canoe ride! Have you ever been in a canoe?

Right: These people are having an outdoor meal of sausages.

Opposite: On Midsummer's Day at midnight, people light bonfires made from twigs and leaves. They dance, have barbecues, and stay up late to enjoy the bright night.

During Midsummer, a special pole is set up in the villages or towns where Swedish-speaking Finns live. People dance around the pole and enjoy themselves.

Think about this
Midsummer is a very special Finnish holiday. Particularly during this time, people are very proud to be Finns. To show how proud they are, they fly their national flag. The Finnish flag is distinctive, white with a blue cross. In the United States, when do Americans show their pride by flying their flag? What is the flag called in the United States?

Midsummer decorations

Finns who cannot take time off to go to the countryside try to create a festive atmosphere in their homes, offices, and factories. They buy birch leaves and lilacs in the markets and put them up as decorations. Even the trains, buses, and trams are decorated with birch branches in Midsummer.

Crayfish parties in Midsummer

Midsummer is also a time for **crayfish** parties for families and friends. At the end of July or beginning of August, people get together in the backyards of their homes to enjoy crayfish and the first days of summer. July 21st marks the official day for crayfish fishing. Only crayfish that are over 4 inches (10 centimeters) long can be caught. Otherwise, they must be thrown back into the sea. Crayfish parties are held in the evening.

A table is laid with **dill**, beer, toast, and schnapps. The crayfish is served after it has been boiled in a pot. Crayfish meat is placed on a piece of toast topped with dill, and downed with beer or schnapps.

INDEPENDENCE DAY

The Finnish Independence Day is celebrated on December 6th. On that day in 1917, Finland became an independent republic. It is an important day for Finns because they were under the rule of other countries for a long time—Sweden from 1200 to 1809 and then Russia from 1809 to 1917. After 717 years of foreign rule, the Finnish people became free, and they are very proud of this.

At the presidential palace ball in 1994, President Martti Ahtisaari and his wife, Eeva Ahtisaari, welcome their guests.

The Finnish remember the soldiers who fought for independence and lost their lives. Prayers are said at church services held on Independence Day. In homes, the lights are switched off and blue-and-white candles are lit. They are placed on windowsills in remembrance. This little boy is lighting the special candles.

The Finns value their freedom tremendously. Here, a Finnish flag with its distinctive blue cross is being raised.

Children and flags

On the eve of Independence Day, children in schools have a special history lesson on how Finland achieved independence. You will know Independence Day has arrived when you see the Finnish blue-and-white flag decorating the windows of many shops. Bakeries sell cakes specially decorated with blue-and-white icing.

The presidential palace ball

The highlight of Independence Day is the presidential palace ball. It is a grand reception held in the evening at the palace of the President of Finland. The people invited to this glittering event are ministers, ambassadors from foreign countries, and even ordinary people the president has met during his visits to various parts of the country. Everyone dresses up to look their best. A dance marks the end of the evening.

Above: Students participating in the torch parade reach Senate Square.

Students' torch parade

The biggest celebrations on Independence Day are held in Helsinki, the capital of Finland. Celebrations begin at nine in the morning with a flag-raising ceremony. This is followed by a church service. In the evening, students hold a torch parade. After lighting candles on the graves at Hietaniemi Graveyard, where past presidents are buried, the students walk to Senate Square.

Think about this

When does your country celebrate its independence? What is this day called, and what do people do on that day? Do you know the significance of your country's independence day? Do you feel proud of your country whenever you celebrate its independence?

Opposite: Like other countries, Independence Day in Finland is a time for people to display their **patriotism**, or national pride. Glorious fireworks in the sky are part of the celebrations on Independence Day.

CHRISTMAS

D o you know why Christmas is celebrated in Finland? A long time ago, on the darkest day of the year (December 23rd), the Finns had finished their harvesting. However, food had to be collected and stored to last the entire long, cold winter. The people decided to have a feast before the hardship began. They called this festival *joulu* [YO-lo]. When Christianity arrived in Finland, the festival became more of a religious celebration—called Christmas.

Saint Stephen's Day falls on December 26th. On this day, children ride in the snow on a sleigh pulled by a foal or young horse. This is to remember Saint Stephen, the patron saint of horses.

Santa's helpers wear red clothes with red caps. They help Santa make and give away toys.

Announcing the Christmas Peace

Christmas officially begins in Finland when the Christmas Peace is announced on Christmas Eve over the radio in Turku. Turku is the old capital of Finland. The idea of the Christmas Peace started 500 years ago, when the Finnish government declared that anyone who behaved badly during the 12 days of Christmas would be punished more heavily than usual. The Christmas Peace is still made nowadays.

Above: On Christmas Eve, the Finnish enjoy a **sauna** before having dinner.

Below: It is easy to overeat at Christmas with such scrumptious dishes!

Celebrating Christmas in a Finnish family

After hearing the Christmas Peace on radio, children join their families to have lunch, which is usually a meal of rice porridge. At five o'clock in the evening, families visit the graves of their relatives who have passed away. Lighted candles are placed on the graves in their memory. At six o'clock, families go to church.

Above: Christmas is a time for remembering loved ones, including those who have passed away.

Below: Building a snowman is fun, but it takes a lot of effort. These two children are hard at work.

Santa Claus Village

In Rovaniemi, which is in Lapland, there is a Santa Claus Village. There is always someone dressed as Santa Claus to greet visitors. He is happiest when he sees children. He has a workshop in the village where his helpers make toys and gifts. Children who cannot visit Santa Claus write a letter to him, and he always replies.

Who is Joulupukki?

After attending the church service on Christmas Eve, children get ready for the most exciting part of Christmas. Santa Claus actually pays a visit and gives away presents! He is called *Joulupukki* [YO-lo-POO-kee], or yule buck. Santa Claus lives in Korvatunturi in Lapland with his helpers.

Children look forward to Christmas, when they can sing Christmas carols with joy. This choir is ready for their concert to begin.

Think about this
Christmas is a family occasion. So, many weeks before Christmas, people who know each other at work or school gather to have *pikkujoulu* [pee-KOO-yo-lo], or "little Christmas" parties. Friends also use these gatherings to make Christmas decorations together.

23

LUCIA DAY

Imagine waking your parents on a cold winter's day with a cheerful song and a breakfast tray! That is what young Swedish girls do on December 13th—Lucia Day. On this special day, the daughter in the family brings coffee to her parents while they are still in bed.

She dresses in a white robe with a red belt and wears a crown of candles. She sings as she makes her entry into their room to wake them up. If she has brothers and sisters, they will also dress up and sing along with her.

Special candles and calendars are used during Advent.

Who is Lucia?

Lucia was a young girl who lived on the island of Sicily in Italy. One thousand and six hundred years ago, Lucia was burned to death because of her Christian **faith**. She was eventually declared a saint. The white robe worn on Lucia Day represents innocence; the red belt, the blood Lucia shed as a **martyr**; and the crown, her holiness.

This is the white robe, red belt, and crown of candles worn on Lucia Day.

Advent

Lucia Day falls in the middle of Advent. There are four Advent Sundays altogether. The last Advent Sunday is the Sunday just before Christmas. To count the days to Christmas, children hang up their Advent calendars. These calendars have 24 pockets representing each day of the month until December 24th. Families also count the days to Christmas with the help of Advent candles. The first candle is lit on the first Advent Sunday, then this candle and a second candle on the second Sunday, and so on until the fourth candle is lit on the fourth Sunday, forming a slanting row.

Advent concerts

The Christmas season begins with the first Sunday of Advent. This is the beginning of the Advent concert season in churches and singing halls. It is also a time when Christmas lights come on in shops and offices. All the towns in Finland are brightly lit, taking on a festive atmosphere.

In Pietarsaari, a town on the western coast of Finland, there is even a Christmas street called Storgatan. This street has been decorated since the 1840s. Hung above the street are three giant decorations: a cross to represent faith, an anchor signifying hope, and a heart representing love.

On Lucia Day, people dig holes in the snow, place lighted candles in the holes, and put snowballs over the hole. The light that shines through makes a very pretty sight.

THINGS FOR YOU TO DO

Easter means that spring is coming. To help tell when spring arrives, children in Finland grow grass from rye seeds. They place the pot or plate of planted seeds on a windowsill. They also make toy chicks and place decorated eggs next to a vase of willow twigs. When the willow twigs bud (becoming pussy willows) and the green grass grows, the children know spring has arrived, and the happy Easter holidays will begin.

Make your own Finnish Easter scene

To do this, you will need yellow cotton wool balls, yellow cardboard, a brown felt-tip marker, a pair of scissors, and some green felt. Ask an adult to help you draw the shape of a chick's head on the yellow cardboard. The shape of a chick's head is like a hen's, except smaller. Draw six such shapes and cut them out. Next, make a vertical cut into each chick's neck; insert and glue a small yellow cotton ball. Color the beak with the marker, and dot the eyes. Cut out a small square of green felt and place the chicks on their carpet of "grass."

Make a Christmas gnome from a napkin

The Christmas gnome is one of Santa's many helpers. The Finns call him *tontut* [ton-TOOT]. He helps Santa make toys for children all over the world. In Finland, children know tontut is watching them to find out if they have been good or bad and if they deserve to receive presents at Christmas. What does tontut look like? Follow the instructions below and find out!

First, take a square red napkin and fold in the corners as shown in the picture. The tips of the folded corners should meet in the center of the napkin at the back. Using a piece of sticky tape, tape these four tips down.

Then, cut a piece of white felt. This is for the gnome's face and beard. Cut the edge of the white felt in straight lines so that the gnome can have his beard.

Cut a nose out of red felt and two eyes out of black felt, then glue them onto the gnome's face. If you want to draw the eyes on yourself, all the better! Finally, fold back both sides of the excess white felt and glue them down. Now, you have your very own gnome!

Things to look for in your library

A Short History of Finland. Fred Singleton (Cambridge University Press, 1990).

Finland. (Enchantment of the World. Second Series). Sylvia McNair (Children's Press, 1997).

Finland: Fresh and Original. (video).

Finland is Color. (video).

The Land and People of Finland. Patricia Lander (Lippincott-Raven Publishers, 1989).

The Magic Storysinger: A Tale from the Finnish Epic Kalevala. M. E. A. McNeil (Fromm International, 1993).

The Maiden of Northland: A Hero Tale of Finland. Aaron Shepard (Atheneum, 1996).

Traditional Finnish Festivities. (http://www.vn.fi/um/finfo/english/juhlaeng.html, 1993).

MAKE A GNOME'S HAT

Santa Claus always has helpers who wear red hats. Today, Finnish children wear these red hats when they help their parents decorate the Christmas tree. You can make a red hat, too! Put it on the next time you help decorate the Christmas tree in your home.

You will need:
1. Red felt 26" x 18" (66 x 46 cm)
2. Green felt 12" x 9" (30 x 23 cm)
3. Scissors
4. A wax pencil
5. Glue
6. Stapler
7. Staples
8. Styrofoam ball
9. Ball of white thread

2 Staple both triangles together. Turn the hat inside out.

1 Fold the red felt in half lengthwise. With the thread, measure all around your head and divide this length by two. Add 2 inches (5 cm). Using the wax pencil, mark out the new measurement on the bottom edge of the felt. Draw two long lines to meet at the top edge, forming a triangle as shown in the picture. Cut along the lines to get two felt triangles.

3 Using the thread, measure the base length of the hat. Cut out a small rectangle of this length from the green felt. Glue the green felt onto the red hat as shown in the picture. Trim the edges of the green felt to make the hat look neat.

4 Glue the styrofoam ball to the tip of the hat. Now, you have your very own gnome's hat!

MAKE SHROVE TUESDAY BUNS

Eating Shrove Tuesday buns before Easter is a tradition. Some Finns eat the special buns as a dessert in hot milk. Others cut the bun in half, fill the bottom slice with whipped cream, and put the top back again. Whichever way you eat it, the bun is delicious.

You will need:

1. ½ cup (100 g) butter
2. ½ cup (100 g) sugar
3. ⅔ cup (160 ml) lukewarm milk
4. ½ tablespoon crushed cardamom
5. ¼ cup (50 g) yeast
6. 3 cups (420 g) flour
7. Whipped cream
8. 2 eggs
9. 1 teaspoon salt
10. Measuring spoons
11. Wooden spoon
12. Measuring cup
13. Whisk
14. Rolling pin
15. Oven mitt
16. Wooden board
17. Cooking brush
18. Butter knife
19. Non-stick baking tray
20. Mixing bowl

1 Dissolve the yeast in the milk. Add in one beaten egg. Put in the salt, sugar, cardamom, and flour, and whisk.

2 Add in butter. Knead the dough with your fingers until it does not stick to the sides of the bowl. Leave the dough alone for 30 minutes at room temperature.

3 Using the rolling pin, flatten the dough into a sheet about ½ inch (1.2 cm) thick. Spread butter on the dough, then roll it up.

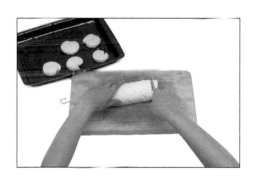

4 Roll the dough.

5 Cut the rolled dough into round pieces and put them on the baking tray. Leave them to rise for about an hour. Break the other egg and beat it. Brush the top of the buns with the egg and bake them at 440°F (225°C) for about 10 minutes. When they have cooled down, cut the buns in half and spread whipped cream over the bottom half. Put the top half back on and your buns are ready!

GLOSSARY

canoeing, 13	A type of sport, using a small paddle to row a long, narrow boat.
crayfish, 14	A shellfish that looks like a small lobster.
Crusades, 4	Holy wars waged by European Christians against Muslims to win back Palestine (the Holy Land) during the 11th, 12th, and 13th centuries.
dill, 14	A sweet-smelling herb used for flavoring.
faith, 24	Belief in the doctrines of a certain religion.
flax, 9	A plant whose stem can be used to make cloth. Its seeds are used to produce linseed oil.
martyr, 24	A person who dies for his or her religious beliefs.
patriotism, 18	Love and loyalty for one's own country.
pikkujoulu, 23	"Little Christmas" parties, when people get together to prepare cakes and decorations for the coming Christmas.
sauna, 21	A small room containing wooden benches and a stove with heated stones.

INDEX

Picture credits
Camera Press: 9, 12 (both), 20 (bottom), 25 (bottom); Comma Finland: 4, 13 (top), 14 (top); Fennopress Oy: 8 (bottom), 22 (top); Kuvasuomi Ky Matti Kolho: 7 (top), 10 (both), 11, 15, 20 (top), 21 (both), 22 (bottom), 26; Lehtikuva Oy: 1, 2, 3 (both), 7 (bottom), 8 (top), 14 (bottom), 16 (both), 17, 18, 19, 23, 24 (both), 25 (top), 28; Life File: 5, 6; David Simson: 13 (bottom)